The Story of Science

Early Humans

by Roy A. Gallant

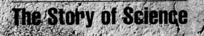

BENCHMARK BOOKS

Series Editor: Roy A. Gallant

Series Consultants:

LIFE SCIENCES
Dr. Edward J. Kormondy
Chancellor and Professor of Biology (retired)
University of Hawaii—Hilo/West Oahu

PHYSICAL SCIENCES
Dr. Jerry LaSala, Chairman
Department of Physics
University of Southern Maine

Benchmark Books
Marshall Cavendish Corporation
99 White Plains Road
Tarrytown, NY 10591-9001

Library of Congress Cataloging-in-Publication Data
Gallant, Roy A.
     Early Humans/ by Roy A. Gallant.
        p. cm. — (The story of science series)
Includes bibliographical references and index.
Summary: Discusses human evolution and the search for the earliest forms of humans, examin-ing the Neanderthals, Homo erectus, the variety of fossils found in Africa, and the early apelike hominids.
ISBN 0-7614-0960-2
        1. Human evolution—Juvenile literature. 2. Fossil hominids—Juvenile literature. [1. Fossil hominids. 2. Evolution. 3. Fossils. 4. Paleontology.] I. Title. II. Series: Gallant, Roy A. Story of science series .
GN281..G25   1999   599.93'8—dc21   98-28037   CIP   AC

Photo research by Linda Sykes
Diagrams on pp. 9, 20, 53, 62, 64, 66–67 by Jeannine L. Dickey
Picture credits: The photographs in this book are used by permission of and through the courtesy of: © National Geographic: cover, 27, 30-31, 37, 58(Kenneth Garrett). © Natural History Museum, London: 6, 10, 23, 55(right), 65. © English Heritage Photo Library: 12(on behalf of the Darwin Heirlooms Trust). © Photo Researchers: 14(John Reader), 45(George Gerster). © Bruce Coleman, Inc.: 17(Joy Spurr), 29. © John Prag: 18 (top), 18 (bottom)(University of Manchester). © AKG Photo, London:title page, 24, 25. © Ira Block: 26. © Margo Crabtree: 41, 49, 50. © Institute of Human Origins: 55 (inset). © American Museum of Natural History: 60 (inset). © Roy Gallant: 60, 61, 69 (right). © Lee Foster: 69 (left).

Printed in Hong Kong
6 5 4 3 2 1

Cover: Perhaps more has been written about Neandertal Man than about any others on our ancestral tree. Prominent browridges set Neandertals apart from us, but in many other ways they were much like us. Neandertals lived in Europe from about 230,000 to 30,000 years ago. Their origin may go back 300,000 years. Among questions about them still being asked are: Where did they come from? And why did they suddenly die out without as much as a whisper of cause?

For Jeannine

The more the secrets of Nature are probed,
the greater the wonder that they instill.

—Sir Gavin de Beer, 1964

Contents

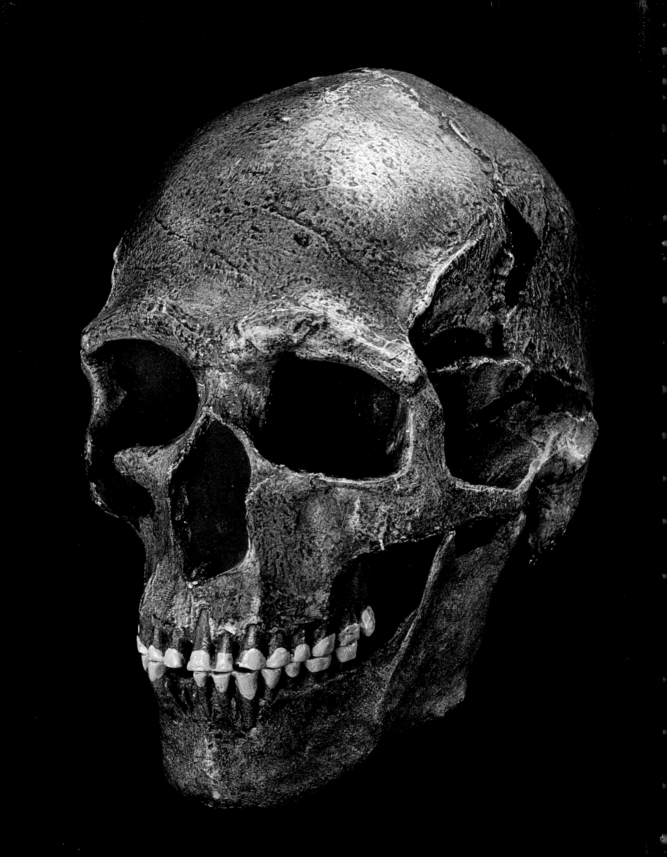

One

Where Did We Come From?

"In the Beginning" for Humans

Where human beings came from, and when, are haunting questions. Some say that we will never know, so why even bother to ask. Others point to their religion and say that the answers can be found there and that we don't have to search further. But there are as many answers as there are religions. So where does one start? (See diagram on page 62 for one start.)

Suppose that you were an ancient Egyptian living some 6,000 years ago. You would have been told that the great Sun god, Ra-Atum, first created himself. Then he created a large family of less powerful gods. All people came into being with these lesser gods as their ancestors. We call such stories "creation myths."

A creation myth of the Yuchi Indians of eastern Tennessee

This Cro-Magnon skull is some 30,000 years old. Unearthed in Czechoslovakia, it is classified as Homo sapiens. Cro-Magnon people were so much like us that you wouldn't give one a second look if he sat down beside you on a bus.

also casts the Sun in the role of a creator god. As the Sun first rose and moved across the sky, it cast a beautiful light over the land and let fall a drop of blood. From that blood, and the earth where it fell, came the first people. They were the Yuchi Indians. They called themselves Tsohaya, "People of the Sun." Every man who took that name had a picture of the Sun on his door. Two thousand years ago people living in Armenia, a country in eastern Europe, worshiped their Sun god, Aramazd. They called themselves "Children of the Sun."

In those long ago days, before science became a way of thinking about the world, myths played an important role. They provided answers to many questions that even the wisest thinkers could not answer: the apparent passage overhead of the Moon, Sun, and stars, the sprouting of seeds, the fire of meteors, and the beginning of all forms of living things. Supernatural powers—gods and demons—could shape and reshape the world as they chose. If belief in the supernatural did not lead to enlightenment, it at least provided peace of mind. In the language of science today, we would say that the invention of myths provided a model to help explain what people could observe of the world but could not understand. For as long as the myth model worked, fine. But there came a time when some people wanted sounder explanations of the world, a time when the old myths no longer seemed convincing.

In the Western world that time came in Greece around 600 B.C. Several schools of philosophers blossomed over the centuries. Their names fill our books of ancient history—Plato, Aristotle, Empedocles, and many others. They began to search for natural causes to account for the formation of the world and its living forms. It was these men who were to lay early foundation stones for modern science.

Fossils: Links with the Past

Another of those early Greek scholars was one named Xeno-phanes. Born around 560 B.C., he took a special interest in *fossils*, the ancient remains of animals and plants, as clues to past life. He found fossils of fish far inland. Many people wondered how a fish fossil could end up on a mountainside far from the ocean. He said that in the dim past, parts of the land had been covered by sea. Later the land beneath the sea was thrust up as a mountain range and so left the fish fossils high and dry. Around A.D. 500—during the years called the Dark Ages—many people believed that fossils were the work of the devil when he tried unsuccessfully to create animals.

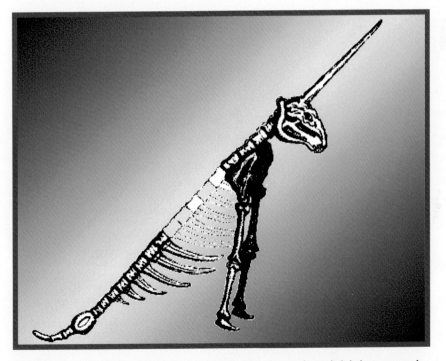

Fossils are keys to past life. But early fossil hunters often didn't know much about the bones they uncovered. In 1749 Von Guericke assembled odds and ends of unrelated fossil bones to reconstruct the mythical beast called a unicorn, with a horn in the middle of its forehead.

Another to take up the serious study of fossils was the Italian Leonardo da Vinci, who lived around 1500. He was a remarkable man—a painter, inventor, engineer, musician, and scientist. He, too, had found fossils of sea animals high among the mountains of northern Italy. He explained that after the animals died and sank to the bottom of the sea, they were covered over by mud and other *sediments* washed off the land. The sediments eventually turned into rock, and later the old sea floor was uplifted as land. Wearing away of the rock eventually exposed the fossils.

A man whose long name matched his important work in science was Baron Georges Jean-Léopold-Nicolas-Frédéric Cuvier. Cuvier became the founder of paleontology, the science that studies past life on the basis of fossils. Cuvier lived from 1769 to 1832.

As early as the 1600s, scientists knew that older layers of rock usually are covered by younger layers. So the deeper the rock layer, the older the fossils the rock layers contain. Around 1800 the French naturalist and geologist Georges Cuvier was studying the fossil-bearing rock layers around Paris. As he arranged his fossils in the same order as the rocks containing them, he discovered something important: the fossils changed in an orderly way from layer to layer. Those deep down from older rock layers were less like their modern living relatives. Those in the younger rock layers higher up were more like their living relatives. Cuvier became the first to relate the structure of fossil animals to their then-living relatives. He became the founder of the science of *paleontology*, the science that studies past life on the basis of fossils.

Darwin and Evolution

Cuvier's work produced strong evidence for something else, but something he refused to accept—that animals and plants change over long periods of geologic time. It was an idea that had been around for many years, but one that few scientists had yet come to accept. Then came the year 1859. The English naturalist Charles Darwin published a book that shook the worlds of science and religion alike. On its first day of publication all 1,250 copies of the book were sold. In it Darwin presented page after page of evidence that plants and animals change biologically over time. Such a notion contradicted that monument of authority for nearly 2,000 years, the Bible. That was one reason why so many were shocked by Darwin's book.

The book had the long title of *The Origin of Species by Means of Natural Selection; or, the Preservation of Favored Races in the Struggle for Life.* It told its readers what *every* geologist had known for some time: that what is now land had once been covered by vast inland seas; that long periods of cold had gripped parts of Europe and North America and covered them with great ice sheets; that tropical forests could change into deserts, and sections of the ocean floor could be thrust up as mountains. In the face of such changes, the book said, many *species* of animals and plants would not be able to cope. They would perish in the new harsh conditions. After all, its was common knowledge that the mastodons and many other species had not been able to cope with the environmental change at the end of the last ice age some 10,000 years ago.

Countless millions of species over *geologic time* likewise had died out and become *extinct*, gone the way of the passenger pigeon, the flightless dodo bird, and the dinosaurs. More than 99 percent of all the species that have ever lived on Earth are now extinct. Yet over time new species have always evolved and been in tune with the changed environmental conditions. But a few species, such as the horseshoe crab and the ginkgo tree, have survived almost unchanged for millions of years.

How do new species evolve? The secret lies in a change in the genes of one or more members of a population. Genes are those biological units of inheritance that we get from our parents that make us appear the way we do, having black or brown hair, blue or brown eyes, being tall or short, and so on. Such gene changes are called *mutations*. Although most mutations are harmful, some have helped equip an individual to cope with a major change in the environment. Such a mutation change might have resulted in a longer reach, a swifter gait to escape a predator, thicker fur for warmth, or a better brain. Those mutant individuals that became more fit than their less fortunate companions survived the environmental change. By surviving, they lived to pass on to their offspring their improved gene makeup. Over millions of years, Darwin told his readers, species of plants and animals change in a process called *evolution*.

At the time, most people had been taught to believe that species never change. They believed that the dog species or domestic cat species had always been exactly the same, as had all other species, including humans. Some scientists of

Charles Robert Darwin, an English naturalist, who lived from 1809 to 1882, developed the principle of evolution through natural selection. The idea turned the science of biology upside down in the mid-1800s. Today Darwin's basic ideas about how species evolve are accepted the world over. This portrait of Darwin at age 31 was painted by George Richmond.

the 1800s even refused to accept the fossil evidence that species become extinct.

Evolutionists before Darwin

Darwin was not the first to say that species evolve. Nearly a hundred years earlier, the French scientist George-Louis Leclerc de Buffon maintained that changes in Earth's environment somehow brought about structural changes in plants and animals. At the time, no one knew how such beneficial changes were passed on from parent to offspring. But it was clear that such changes *were* passed on. Buffon argued in favor of evolution by showing that many animals have useless parts, such as the tailbone in human beings. He further took the bold step to say that Earth had existed for millions of years. The statement was bold because it contradicted the biblical date of creation of 4004 B.C.

Also in the 1700s, Darwin's grandfather, Erasmus Darwin, said that millions of years ago there had been a primitive parent organism that had given rise to all living things. Over those millions of years, he said, the countless offspring of the original parent kept changing, improving by becoming more fit, and evolving into forms more and more like today's plants and animals.

Although Charles Darwin's basic idea about evolution was not new, his version was supported by mountains of evidence. And that evidence was very hard to reject on scientific grounds. Today virtually *every* biologist the world over accepts the idea of evolution as solid fact. But there is much discussion, and disagreement, among biologists about the *ways* evolution works. That point is well made when we look into the work of *paleontologists* trying to unravel the complex story of how our human species evolved. Because they are searching for the roots of our biological and cultural beginnings, they are called *paleoanthropologists*.

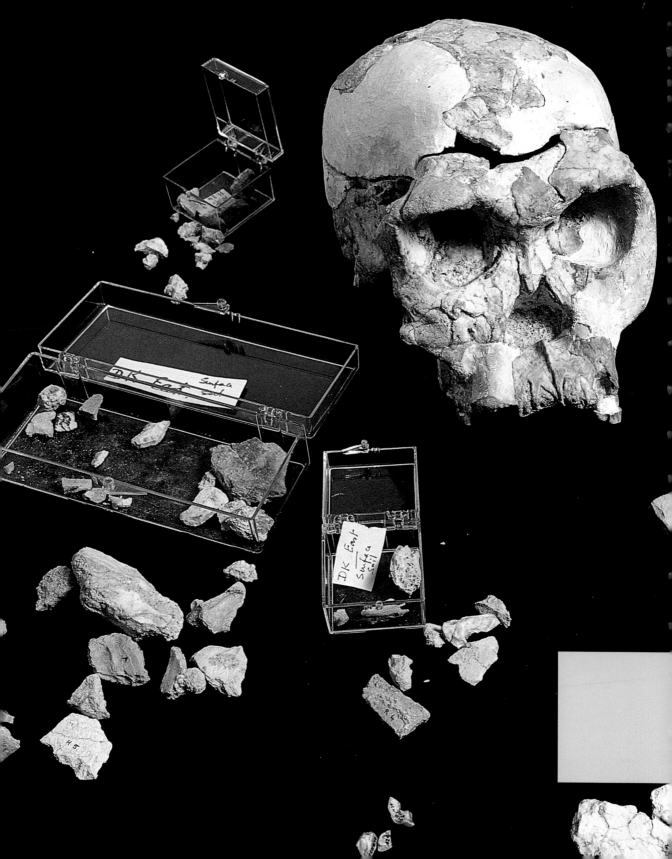

Two

The Making of the Puzzle

Keepers of the Bones

The fossil human bones are priceless. They lie in cabinet drawers in about a dozen museums around the world, and they are never shown to the public for fear of theft or damage. Most are small fragments about the size of your thumbnail or a silver dollar. Sometimes the cap section of a skull is found, but more often it is a smaller piece of the skull, or a toe bone, lots of teeth. Surprisingly often an entire detached lower jawbone is found.

Only scientists who study how, when, and where our ancestors of thousands and millions of years ago evolved are allowed

(Continued on page 19)

Most fossil bone fragments of early humans, and our ancestors, are the size of your thumb or a silver dollar. A scientist finding such fossil remains then faces the task of piecing them together, which can take months. With luck, and enough bone fragments, an ancient skull can be reconstructed. The missing pieces may then be patched in with plaster or some other material. The skull shown here is that of Homo habilis, *who lived about two million years ago.*

Earth's rocky crust is a vast graveyard of fossil remains of animals and plants that have lived at one time or another throughout most of Earth's geologic history. The word *fossil* comes from the Latin *fossilis*, which means "dug up." Fossils are the remains of animals and

How Fossils Are Formed

plants that have died and been buried by sediments—sand, mud, or clay, for example. After long periods of time deep layers of ocean floor sediments may be pressed to form rock. Later the rock may be exposed to the air when the old sea dries up. *Erosion* by rain and wind may then wear away the rock and expose the fossils.

Many of the animals that are now part of the fossil record were preserved as their bones were changed into something different. Water containing minerals slowly seeping down through sediments was soaked up by the porous bone. As the water gradually evaporated, the minerals were left behind and filled the small open spaces within the bone. Brightly colored minerals such as silica, calcite, or orange and red iron materials often become part of a fossil bone. In some petrified wood, silica has not only filled in small hollow spaces, but has replaced the once-living woody tissue. This has happened so perfectly that the individual cells and annual tree rings show up in beautiful detail millions of years later. Most fossils are preserved in the sedimentary rocks known as sandstone, limestone, and shale.

In a few unusual cases, some very special condition may preserve almost the entire animal. Fossil mammoths have been found preserved in frozen ground, completely refrigerated for more than 25,000 years in Siberia and Alaska. In South America parts of mummified ground sloths have been found preserved in dry and protected caves. And insect fossils have been found perfectly preserved in amber. The insect became fossilized when it got stuck and encased in the oozing pitch of a tree. The pitch then solidified as amber.

Many plant and animal fossils were formed by a process called mineral replacement. Millions of years ago this petrified log was formed as the tree died and was buried in sediments. Over centuries, mineral-bearing water seeped down through the sediments and was soaked up by the wood. Gradually the wood was dissolved away and only the colorful hardened minerals were left.

To find out what a fossil skull might have looked like when its owner was alive, technicians insert pegs to mark the depth of face tissue. Artificial eyes are then inserted in the eye sockets and modeling materials are smoothed over the bone and built up until they cover the pegs. Here, artist Richard Neave reconstructs the face of an Iron Age female skull named Yde Girl. The final result is shown at right.

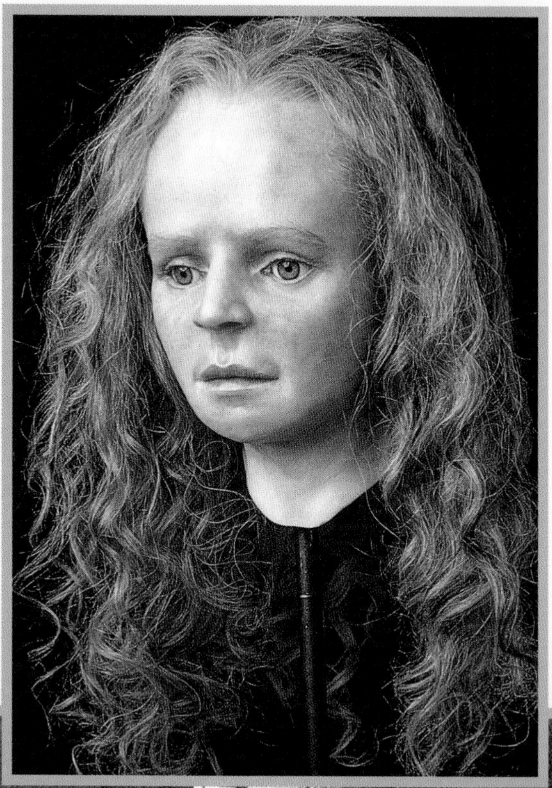

to handle those priceless fossil bones. Many museums exhibit fossil human skulls, or a piece of fossilized human leg bone that may be a million or so years old. But what you see are plaster or plastic copies of the original fossils. Rarely is a fossil skull complete. Almost always it must be reconstructed bit by bit, like the pieces of a jigsaw puzzle, from dozens of tiny original fragments. The missing pieces are then patched in with some other material, colored to show that they are not part of the original. All original pieces are kept in safes with massive steel doors that remind you more of a bank than a museum storage room.

Dubois Finds His "Ape-Man"

By the late 1880s Darwin's thoughts on evolution had gained much attention around the world. In 1871 he had published his book *The Descent of Man*. In it he described in great detail the common patterns in body plan between apes, humans, and other species. He clearly showed that humans, right along with all the other creatures in the animal kingdom, also had evolved. He further stated that apes and humans had evolved from a common ancestor long, long before.

One person who found Darwin's ideas not only fascinating, but very convincing, was a young Dutch military doctor named Eugène Dubois. He was so won over by Darwin that he was determined to find the "missing link" between apes and humans. By the late 1880s only about a half dozen fossils of humans were known, but that was enough to convince Dubois that his search would be worthwhile. So in 1887 he sailed from Holland to Java, which is a bit north of Australia.

With the help of fifty convict laborers, he began digging along the shores of the Solo River. Then, near the village of Trinil in 1891, he unearthed the top part of a skull. The next two years'

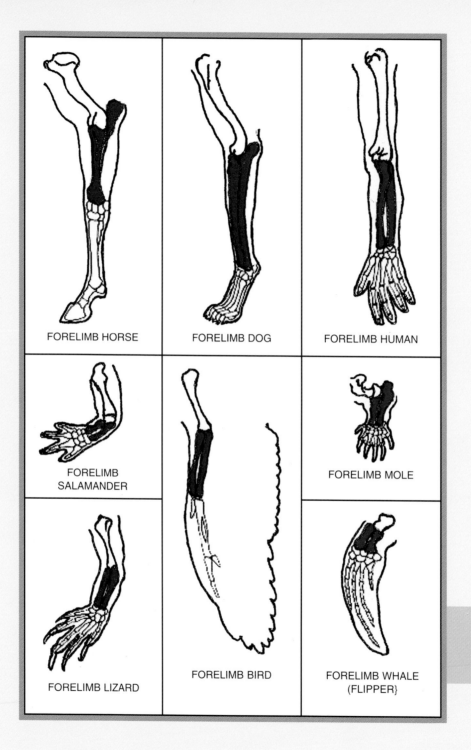

FORELIMB HORSE

FORELIMB DOG

FORELIMB HUMAN

FORELIMB
SALAMANDER

FORELIMB MOLE

FORELIMB LIZARD

FORELIMB BIRD

FORELIMB WHALE
(FLIPPER)

work uncovered a molar tooth and part of an upper leg bone. All three fossils seemed to be from some form of early human, not from an ape. For example, the two ends and straightness of the leg bone showed that it came from an animal who walked upright. Dubois's missing-link "ape-man" was later given the scientific name *Homo erectus*, which means "upright man." It became popularly known as Java Man and has been dated at 700,000 years old. The famous *archaeologist* Mary D. Leakey once remarked, "In archaeology you almost never find what you set out to find." Dubois was lucky. He did.

Dubois's remarkable discovery gained world attention and added one more piece to the puzzle of the origin of humans. Thousands of more pieces have been uncovered since Dubois's time, especially since about 1960. All give us fascinating glimpses of the puzzle. All the pieces are related in some way, but some are little islands of mystery. Even so, the larger picture keeps growing and keeps coming into sharper focus. Perhaps the best way to see the puzzle as it has developed since Dubois' time, and earlier, is to start with modern humans. So we will begin with the earliest appearances of people just like us—where their fossil bones and works of art have been found, and how old they are. From there we will push time ever backward in our search for still older humans, and finally the apelike creatures who gave rise to them.

Similarities in the limb bones (in red) of different species show a common pattern. The only logical explanation for that pattern is that horses, dogs, humans, and the other five species shown evolved from a common ancestor.

Three

From Us to the Neandertals

Homo sapiens in Europe

At first, nothing seemed unusual about the skull railroad workers discovered in the Dordogne region of southwestern France in 1868. It had only a slight bulge of bone just above the eyebrow region. That bony feature marked the skull as that of a modern human being. What turned out to be unusual about the skull was its age—between 13,000 and 20,000 years old. It was popularly called "Cro-Magnon," after the rock shelter where the skull was found. Its scientific name is the same as ours—*Homo sapiens*, which means "wise man." Cro-Magnon people were so much like us that you wouldn't give one a second look if he sat down beside you on a bus.

Cro-Magnon tools were made with skill and a sense of design. The items shown here were made about 30,000 years ago. From left to right: a bone used to make needles; a finished needle; two harpoon heads; and two decorative human heads carved from a mammoth's ivory tusk.

These versions of modern humans seem to have not known permanent shelters. Rather they were hunter-gatherers who followed their favorite food animals and ate wild berries, sweet roots, and other nourishing vegetation that happened to be growing at the time. They were not farmers, and they did not have domesticated animals. We know that they were highly skilled hunters because fossil bones of reindeer, mammoth, and bison have been found along with their bones. The ability to hunt such large and powerful animals required that several hunters work together. Such a cooperative effort meant an ability to plan the hunt and to shout meaningful instructions as the hunters stalked the animal and then moved in for the kill. So Cro-Magnon people must have had a well-developed language, although we will never know what it sounded like.

Artists and Musicians

Cro-Magnon people also fashioned tools out of stone, ivory, bone, and wood. Many of the tools and carvings are exquisitely made. And they were fine artists. By torchlight, deep inside limestone caves, they decorated the walls and ceilings with strikingly beautiful paintings of the animals they hunted. Their artistic period reached a peak in France and Spain between 18,000 and 9,000 years ago. During that time they decorated some 200 known caves. France's famous Lascaux Cave has about 600 paintings and nearly 1,500 engravings. The purpose of this art was not to pass the time of day or to amaze. It seems to have been deadly serious, a kind of magic that would somehow make

Cro-Magnon people were highly skilled artists who left hundreds of paintings on the walls and ceilings of caves in France and Spain. Their artistic period reached a peak between 18,000 and 9,000 years ago. During that time they

the hunt successful. Paint an image of the animal and it will be easier to kill.

Some of these people seem to have been musicians. Part of a flutelike instrument made of bird bone has been dated at 25,000 years old, but some have questioned whether the makers of the "flute" were that far advanced culturally. In any case, we can regard those people as the dawn people of civilization.

Homo sapiens Elsewhere

At about the time the Lascaux Cave painters lived, equally modern people had populated North and South America as groups called Paleo-Indians, ancestors of today's Native Americans.

decorated some 200 known caves. France's famous Lascaux Cave (painting at left) has about 600 paintings and nearly 1,500 engravings. Similar paintings, such as the one above, can be seen in Altamira, Spain.

They were hunter-gatherers and made tools of stone and bone. According to Robson Bonnichsen, director of Oregon State University's Center for the Study of the First Americans, "For evidence we have the following: flakes of mammoth bone dated greater than 30,000 years old from sites in the Old Crow Basin of the northern Yukon Territory; altered bones from El Cedral, northern Mexico, more than 33,000 years old, and a long sequence of simple flaked tools from Toca do Boqueirao da Pedra Furada, Brazil, extending back to 31,500 years ago."

In 1988 paleoanthropologists working in Israel discovered the fossil bones of about ten early modern humans at a site called Qafzeh Cave. Burned flints chipped into an ancient campfire as the flint was being fashioned into tools turned out to be 92,000 years old. This find pushed back the date for early humans to nearly four times that of the ancient flute player. Where did these people come from, and when? Did they evolve in the Middle East? Or did they evolve somewhere else and later migrate to Israel, Europe, and other parts of the world?

About 270 miles (435 kilometers) east of Cape Town, South Africa, is the Klasies River Mouth Cave, overlooking the sea. Scientists studying the cave have uncovered fossilized parts of upper and lower jaws, skull bone fragments, teeth scattered around, and limb bones. All are convincingly modern human remains, says University of Chicago paleoanthropologist Richard

The age of early toolmakers was pushed back to 92,000 years ago with the discovery in 1988 of fossil bones of modern humans, including the skull shown here, at a site called Qafzeh Cave in Israel. Burned flints, chipped into an ancient campfire as the flint was being fashioned into tools, were also found.

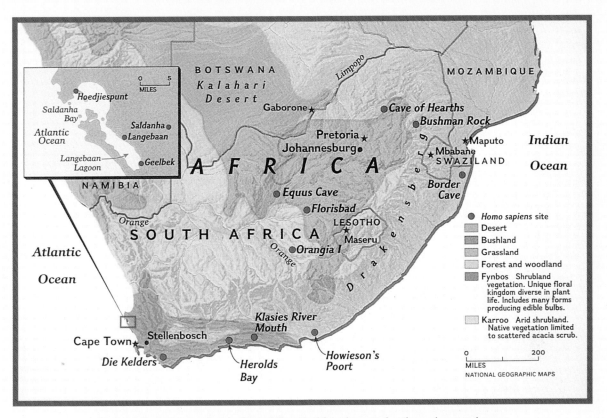

Ancient humans probably found South Africa's grasslands and coastal areas comfortable places to live with a plentiful food supply. Many of the oldest skeletal fossils with modern human features have been found in South Africa.

Klein. Some of the fragments have been dated at between 60,000 and 120,000 years old. If those dates are supported by further such finds, it will push the origin of *Homo sapiens* back some 25,000 years or so still deeper into the past.

Just such support has been found more recently. The site is about 60 miles (96 kilometers) northwest of Cape Town along Langebaan Lagoon. Here human fossil footprints were discovered preserved in rock just by the sea. The rock was dated at 117,000 years old. The footprints were made by a lone figure walking across wet beach sand. Eventually time turned the sand to rock, and the footprints were preserved over those many thousands of years. The prints are so detailed that they could have been made this morning, said one investigator. The big toe impression is clear. So are the arch, the ball, and the heel of the foot. A young teenager today could step into the print and it would fit perfectly. Like the Klasies people, the Langebaan Lagoon people seem quite modern. They probably had language but not as well developed as our own. Nevertheless, it most likely was good enough to allow them to review the events of yesterday and plan tomorrow's activities.

The paleoanthropologist who has investigated and preserved the footprints is Lee Berger, of the University of the Witwatersrand in Johannesburg, South Africa. He is convinced that modern humans first evolved in Africa and then spread northward to other parts of the world.

By about 50,000 years ago *Homo sapiens* had populated virtually all parts of the world—Africa, the Middle East, Europe, Russia, China, India, Malaysia, Indonesia, and Australia, for example. A question we must keep in mind when we describe modern peoples' first appearance in those lands is: How did they get there?

Before we turn the anthropological clock back to still earlier times, to find out who the parents of *Homo sapiens* were, we must examine some other, and very different, humans who were roaming the planet when the Qafzeh, Klasies River Mouth, and Lascaux Cave people were about. There are the Neandertals. Paleoanthropologists are puzzled by them and can't quite figure out just how they relate to us.

A nagging question is how modern people first reached such far-flung lands as the Middle East, Russia, India, China, Indonesia, and Australia. Some 50,000 years ago an Aboriginal artist made this Australian rock painting of a man hunting a kangaroo.

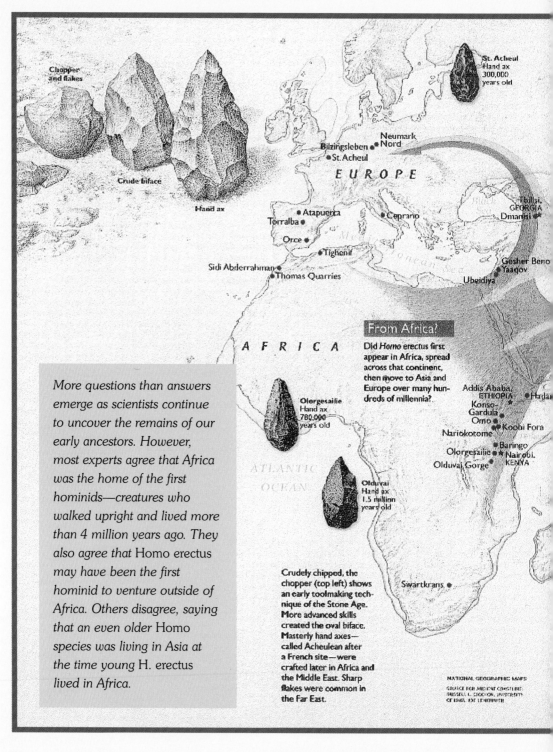

Chopper
and flakes

Crude biface

Hand ax

St. Acheul
Hand ax
300,000
years old

Neumark
Nord
Bilzingsleben
St. Acheul

E U R O P E

Atapuerca
Torralba
Orce
Tighenif
Ceprano

Tbilisi,
GEORGIA
Dmanisi

Sidi Abderrahman
Thomas Quarries

Gesher Beno
Yaaqov

Ubeidiya

A F R I C A

From Africa?

Did *Homo* erectus first
appear in Africa, spread
across that continent,
then move to Asia and
Europe over many hun-
dreds of millennia?

Olorgesailie
Hand ax
780,000
years old

Addis Ababa,
ETHIOPIA
Konso-
Gardula
Omo
Nariokotome
Olorgesailie
Olduvai Gorge

Hadar

Koobi Fora

Baringo
Nairobi,
KENYA

ATLANTIC
OCEAN

Olduvai
Hand ax
1.5 million
years old

More questions than answers
emerge as scientists continue
to uncover the remains of our
early ancestors. However,
most experts agree that Africa
was the home of the first
hominids—creatures who
walked upright and lived more
than 4 million years ago. They
also agree that Homo erectus
may have been the first
hominid to venture outside of
Africa. Others disagree, saying
that an even older Homo
species was living in Asia at
the time young H. erectus
lived in Africa.

Crudely chipped, the
chopper (top left) shows
an early toolmaking tech-
nique of the Stone Age.
More advanced skills
created the oval biface.
Masterly hand axes—
called Acheulean after
a French site—were
crafted later in Africa and
the Middle East. Sharp
flakes were common in
the Far East.

Swartkrans

NATIONAL GEOGRAPHIC MAPS

SOURCE FOR ANCIENT COASTLINE:
RUSSELL L. CIOCHON, UNIVERSITY
OF IOWA, IOC LENOIRIER

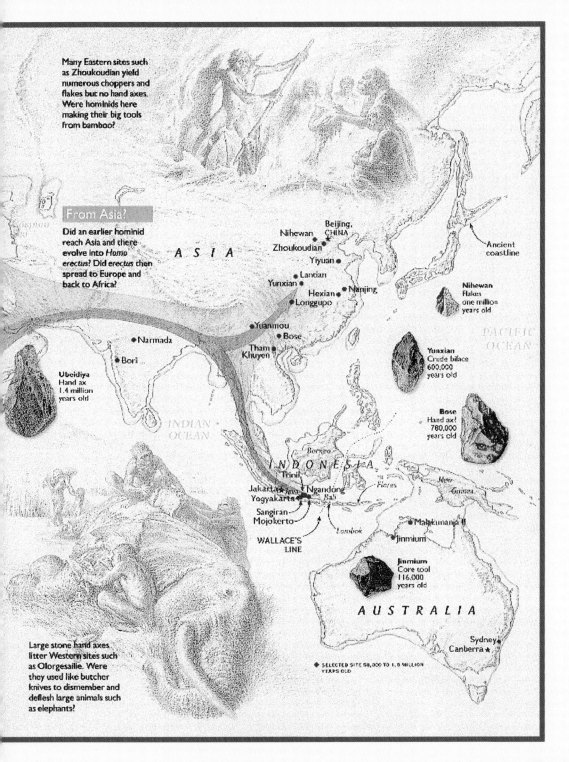

Many Eastern sites such as Zhoukoudian yield numerous choppers and flakes but no hand axes. Were hominids here making their big tools from bamboo?

From Asia?

Did an earlier hominid reach Asia and there evolve into *Homo erectus*? Did *erectus* then spread to Europe and back to Africa?

A S I A

Nihewan
Beijing, CHINA
Zhoukoudian
Yiyuan
Lantian
Yunxian
Hexian
Nanjing
Longgupo
Yuanmou
Bose
Narmada
Tham Khuyen
Bori

Ancient coastline

Nihewan
Flakes one million years old

PACIFIC OCEAN

Yunxian
Crude biface 600,000 years old

Ubeidiya
Hand ax 1.4 million years old

INDIAN OCEAN

Bose
Hand ax? 780,000 years old

I N D O N E S I A
Borneo
Trinil
Jakarta
Yogyakarta
Ngandong
Bali
Sangiran
Mojokerto
Flores
New Guinea

WALLACE'S LINE
Lombok

Malakunanja II
Jinmium

Jinmium
Core tool 116,000 years old

A U S T R A L I A

Sydney
Canberra ★

● SELECTED SITE 50,000 TO 1.8 MILLION YEARS OLD

Large stone hand axes litter Western sites such as Olorgesailie. Were they used like butcher knives to dismember and deflesh large animals such as elephants?

Four

The Mysterious Neandertals

Who Were They?

In 1856 workers were cutting limestone out of Germany's Neander Valley near Düsseldorf. They unearthed a fossil skull and several other bones that seemed to be human, or almost human. At first scientists couldn't agree about what they were. One said the bones were the remains of "some poor idiot or hermit." Others thought they might be the "missing link" between apes and humans. They were called Neandertals. Since their discovery, many more of their bones have come to light, and they continue to cause debate among anthropologists.

The Neandertals roamed overland from Gibraltar in the south to Uzbekistan in the north and lived from about 230,000 to 30,000 years ago. Their origin may go back to 300,000 years. Among questions about them still being asked are: Where did they come from? And why did they suddenly die out without as much as a whisper of cause?

They had short limbs and thick bodies. An adult male stood about 5 feet 6 inches (168 centimeters). Their leg and arm bones were big, evidence that they had tremendous strength. Their skulls were longer than ours and had large brow ridges just over the eyes. They did not have the high foreheads and jutting chins of modern people. Their skulls also show that their brains were a bit larger than ours. Their faces stuck out more than ours do, and they had broad noses and large teeth. Because of those and other differences in *anatomy*, or body plan, these people are called *Homo sapiens* (Neandertal) to tell them apart from *Homo sapiens* (modern). But they also were like us in many ways.

They probably could speak, but perhaps not enough to carry on an involved conversation. They crafted and wore personal ornaments, buried their dead, and took care of injured individuals over long periods. Burials suggest some kind of ritual activity, something not found earlier than the Neandertals. A burial some 60,000 years old, found in Shanidar Cave in Iraq, seems to have included flowers.

The Neandertals were Ice Age people who lived in caves and in tents made of animal skins, but they did not live long by today's standards. Usually they were dead by age thirty. Deep beds of ash found in many of their caves show that they knew how to control fire for warmth and cooking meat. Many of their tools were those of hunters, evidence that they depended on the meat of Ice Age animals for food and on their skins for clothing and shelter. They probably used stout wooden spears with stone points and killed the large Ice Age animals with brute force at close range. There is no evidence that they ever developed the art of throwing a spear from a distance. Thrusting, rather than throwing, a spear was always dangerous.

Some suspect that the Neandertals were cannibals. Cut

marks and unusual breaks in a 50,000-year-old Neandertal skull and limb bones found in a cave in Croatia are evidence. They may have cracked open the bone to eat the marrow. Others think the marks and crushed bones were done as part of a ceremony of some sort.

Were the Neandertals artists? If so, there is little evidence of it. They left no cave paintings, although a carefully polished tooth between 80,000 and 100,000 years old was discovered in Hungary in 1958. The archaeologist who found it says that it was not a tool but was important and must have had some spiritual value.

Many have wondered if the older Neanderthal could be an ancestor of the younger modern humans leading to us. There is nothing in the fossil record to support such a notion. It now seems that they and we evolved from a still earlier group of humans.

Why Did They Die Out?

The Neandertals disappeared suddenly about 30,000 years ago. The mystery has yet to be solved, but there are theories. Bone finds in caves in Israel and France, for example, show that something must have happened over a period of about 10,000 years. There was an overlapping of population territories between the large-jawed Neandertals in Europe and the small-jawed modern humans who lived in the area of Israel, Iraq, and Europe. According to one theory, the culturally advanced Cro-Magnon types might have looked down on the Neandertals as barbarians. Over a period of several thousand years they gradually killed off the Neandertals. If we can learn from the present, ethnic and racial conflict is the rule in many parts of the world. People kill each other because of social, religious, or political differences. It has been like that throughout recorded history. So why should we suppose that human nature was much different even earlier, especially when two different *cultures* shared the same territory and competed for food resources?

Another theory is that Cro-Magnon people entering Europe from the Middle East 40,000 years ago interbred with the Neandertals. So the Neandertal physical features gradually were overwhelmed by Cro-Magnon genes. Nonsense, say others. Fred Spoor, of University College, London, says we have no evidence of interbreeding on a large scale. He adds that Neandertal and Cro-Magnon were two different species and could not produce offspring.

French paleoanthropologist Jacques Hublin thinks that the onset of a colder *climate* 35,000 years ago could have forced the Neandertals southward into warmer Spain. It is there, in scattered caves by the sea, that the last traces of Neandertals are found. A few jawbones and upper leg bones about 33,000 years old, and then nothing. By this time Cro-Magnon types had populated the Americas. And 70,000 years earlier they had proven their skills as seafarers by reaching Australia and Indonesia from China. But those last Neandertals just sat there in some 140 caves on the Rock of Gibraltar, gazing across the few miles of water to a still warmer Africa. Why didn't they make the move to that other land? Were they afraid of the sea? Did they not have the inventiveness to build rafts? Or did they simply lack the curiosity to explore? All we know is that for 200,000 years these large-jawed, ruggedly built people lived. Then they were gone.

The question we must now ask is: Who were the still earlier humans who gave rise to the Neandertals, and to modern *Homo sapiens*?

Five

The Trail Back to *H. erectus*

In 1984 the Spanish paleoanthropologist Juan-Luis Arsuaga began excavating a deep underground cave known as La Sima de los Huesos. The cave is at the back of a large opening at the base of a cliff, and the only way of getting to it is down a 40-foot-deep (12-meter-deep) shaft. What he found there has put one more tiny piece of the puzzle of human origins in place. He thought that he might have found Neandertal's ancestors of some 300,000 years ago. They are the remains of thirty-two teenagers and young adults. The bodies may have been dumped

Exactly when and what routes did early Homo take out of Africa? Entering through Spain or Italy would have meant sea crossings. Were our ancestors of some 700,000 years ago capable of such travel over water? Perhaps some entered Europe from Asia. Permanent settlements north of the Mediterranean Sea might have been discouraged by saber-toothed cats and hyenas until those animals became less plentiful about 500,000 years ago.

down the shaft as a matter of cave cleaning after the youths died.

The bones are from a group called *Homo heidelbergensis*. These people are now thought to have originated in Africa as long ago as 600,000 years. Later they migrated to Spain, where they gave rise to the early Neandertals. Other *heidelbergensis* remains include a lower jawbone discovered in a sand quarry in 1908 at Mauer, near Heidelberg, Germany. It turned out to be 500,000 years old. These older people are not thought to have evolved into *Homo sapiens* (modern). If not, then who gave rise to modern humans?

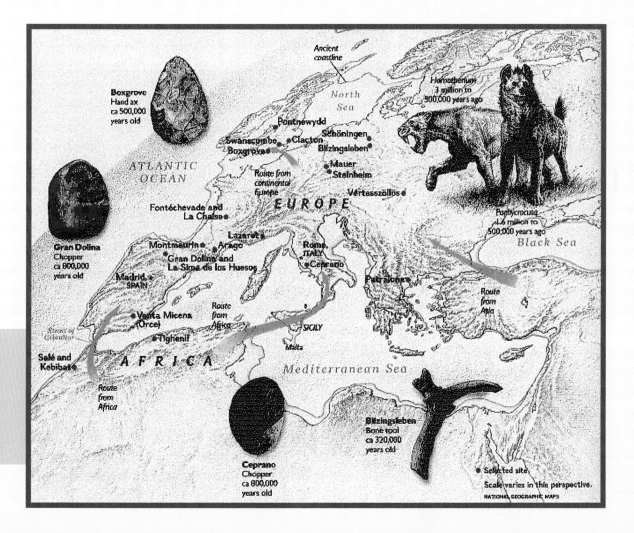

Boxgrove Man

In the spring of 1994 British scientists digging a few miles inland from the English Channel discovered a fossil lower leg bone and hundreds of hand axes at the Boxgrove site. The bone was dated at between 478,000 and 524,000 years old. During that period Britain and France were connected by land, which meant that people from Europe could walk to Britain without having to cross that body of water that today is the English Channel. The human remains, informally called Boxgrove Man, were considered as *Homo heidelbergensis*. A Boxgrove male was nearly 6 feet (183 centimeters) tall and weighed about 200 pounds (91 kilograms). These people were skilled hunters who planned and carried out their kills with expertise guided by language. With the Boxgrove discovery, the British could claim the oldest human in Europe. But not for long.

Soon after, archaeologists digging at Gran Dolina, a site in northern Spain near Burgos, unearthed more than a hundred human bone fragments. There also were 200 stone tools and 300 animal bones, all from an old cave floor. The remains turned out to be more than 780,000 years old. Among the tools was a knife, the oldest known knife found along with human remains in Europe. It was used to butcher animals—deer, horses, elephants. Like the animal bone remains, the human bones at Gran Dolina had cut marks exactly like those discovered at many other sites the world over. The marks are evidence that the people who made them were cannibals, as Neandertal may have been later, and certain U.S. Southwest Indian groups still later.

The Gran Dolina archaeologists now think that their 780,000-year-old humans, which they have named *Homo antecessor*, may be the ones who gave rise to modern humans. If so,

Throughout this book the word *species* is used, and we are about to use the term *genus* as well. What, exactly, do the terms mean, and why bother to use scientific names anyway? They're hard to remember and often hard to say.

One reason is that common names of plants and animals can be confusing. Take the common name *mountain lion* as an example. A mountain lion is also called a *puma*, a *panther*, *mountain cat*, *cougar*, and *catamount*.

What's a Genus?
What's a Species?

To avoid such confusion in biology, all plants and animals are given two scientific names. The first name is called the *genus*, and the second name is called the *species*. Both the genus and species names are always in Latin. Using our mountain lion as an example, here is how it works. All big cats are placed in a large group (the genus) called *Panthera*. Then each different kind of big cat is assigned a species name to further group all those big cats that are alike in their anatomy and that breed together to produce offspring. Lions are classified as *Panthera leo*. Tigers are *Panthera tigris*, and leopards are *Panthera pardus*.

No matter what countries scientists are from, they all use the Latin names for all plants and animals and so avoid confusion. Notice that the genus names always start with a capital letter, while the species names usually do not. Also notice that the two names always appear in italic type. Instead of writing out the genus name, it can be abbreviated as *P. leo* or *P. tigris*, for example.

that would kick heidelbergenses off the human line (see the family tree diagram on page 62).

Who Was Ceprano Man?

In 1994 Spain lost the contest for Europe's first human. In that year Italian archaeologist Italo Biddittu spotted a piece of bone sticking out of an embankment beside a new road about 55 miles (89 kilometers) southeast of Rome. Over the next two years workers collected hundreds more fragments and pieced together a human skullcap. It was called Ceprano Man after a nearby town by that name. To everyone's surprise, the skullcap turned out to be between 800,000 and 900,000 years old. Who were these people who roamed Italy, Spain, Germany, and Britain long before Neandertal appeared there?

Clearly they were a human species and so deserved the genus name tag *Homo*, but not the species name *sapiens*. Biddittu's team members decided to classify their much older Ceprano Man as *Homo erectus*, meaning "upright man," the same name Dubois had given to Java Man. That species had probably evolved in Africa some 2 million years ago and eventually wandered over the globe. Some paleoanthropologists now think that *erectus* may have arrived in Spain a million years ago, becoming the first European and giving rise to *heidelbergensis*.

H. erectus looked much like us, certainly more so than Neandertal. But like Neandertal, *erectus* had protruding brow ridges and a forehead that sloped back. His brain, however, was smaller. *H. erectus* was also more powerfully built than we are. It now seems that *erectus* settled in Java (as Java Man) as early as 1.8 million years ago but for some reason shunned Europe for later settlement. Large numbers of saber-toothed cats, hyenas, and wild dogs may have kept *erectus* away. Before becoming extinct, those dangerous predators roamed Europe between 1.5 million and some 500,000 years ago.

How do we answer our earlier question, "Who were *Homo sapiens'* parents?" So far, we have three candidates—*heidelbergensis*, *antecessor*, and *erectus*. Let's now consider the case for *erectus*.

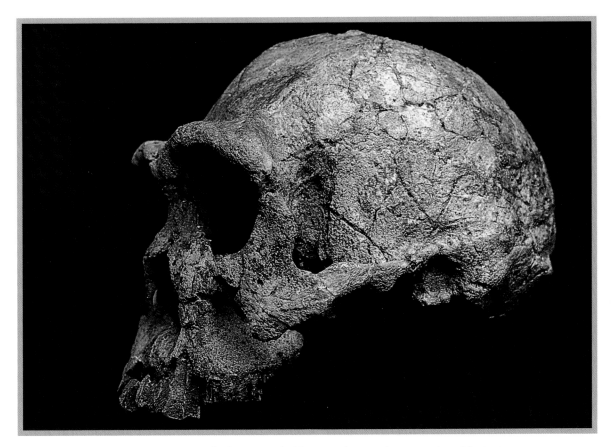

This Homo erectus *skull is remarkably complete and among the oldest, at 1.6 million years of age. Found in Kenya, Africa, it is kept in the National Museum in Nairobi. Notice the big brow ridges, which have virtually disappeared in our modern species.*

41

Six

Globe-Trotting *erectus*

The Turkana Boy

In August 1984 scientists made one of the most remarkable fossil finds in the history of human evolution. It was a nearly complete skeleton of a twelve-year-old boy who lived more than 1.5 million years ago. Its discoverers quickly tagged the boy as *Homo erectus*. However, some other scientists have placed these early "*erectus*" types who lived from 1.8 to 1.4 million years ago in a separate species. They call them *Homo ergaster*, meaning "working man." The boy had stood 5 feet 4 inches (163 centimeters) tall, and his skeleton was almost completely modern. If he had lived to adulthood, he would have reached 6 feet (183 centimeters).

The scientists on the dig were Alan Walker, of Johns Hopkins University, and Richard Leakey, director of the National Museums of Kenya in Nairobi. Their crew was searching for ancient human remains along the west shore of Kenya's Lake

Turkana in Africa. The bones of the Turkana Boy had been trampled by elephants and were scattered about. The skull, which was in seventy pieces, had to be glued back together like pieces of a shattered vase. The boy's bones rested on a layer of volcanic ash that was dated at 1.65 million years old. Although the fossil bones themselves could not be dated directly, their age could be told by the age of the volcanic ash they rested on.

One important improvement that *erectus* enjoyed over those who lived before him was a larger brain. The increase in brain size gave him a major evolutionary leap. The average size of an *erectus* brain was about 1,000 milliliters (about 2 pints), compared with about 1,400 milliliters (about 3 pints) for our brains. A larger brain could mean some ability for speech, and seemingly a sense of curiosity to explore what lies on the other side of the mountain. A better brain also could be useful for *adaptation*, or adjustment, to new environments that demanded cleverness and invention for survival. And it apparently enabled *erectus* to control fire, judging from charcoal hearths found at many sites. The control of fire, in turn, meant that cooked meat could be added to the diet.

Another new feature that seems to arrive on the scene with *erectus* was the invention of the hand axe. It was a stone tool that could cut, scrape, or batter, depending on how it was held. One writer has called it the "Swiss army knife of the day." The oldest known hand axes in the world come from Konso-Gardula, a site in Ethiopia near Kenya. The tools are between 1.37 and 1.7 million years old. Such tools enabled *erectus* to cut away flesh from the bones of a buffalo and then smash the bones to suck out the nutritious tender marrow inside. There is some evidence that *erectus* did the same thing to his fellow creatures, a still earlier instance of cannibalism. Possible evidence has been found in a skeleton dug up at the African site Koobi Fora, on the eastern shore of Lake Turkana.

The Lake Turkana region of Africa is rich in fossils. Since 1968 more than two hundred fossil humans have been found there. Among them is a 1.5-million-year-old *erectus* skull and bone fragments unearthed in 1971. *Erectus* remains have been found in East, South, and North Africa. More, however, have been found in China, Southeast Asia, and India. A question that has still to be answered is this: Are the *erectus* fossils found in Asia the same as the African *erectus* fossils? Some scientists say no, and they are the ones who call the early "*erectus*" African fossils *Homo ergaster*.

Time is one of the puzzling things about the two species. Fossils of an *erectus* girl six years old were discovered in Indonesia in 1936 not far from where Dubois discovered his Java Man. Paleoanthropologist Carl Swisher, of the University of California at Berkeley, dated the bones at 1.8 million years. Other *erectus* fossils have been dated at 1.6 million years. This was the same time the Turkana Boy was playing by his lake. Scientists now wonder how quickly *Homo* (whether *erectus* or *ergaster*) could have left home and reached China and Southeast Asia. And could China be the birthplace of early *Homo* species?

Meet Peking Man

We now move to China and back to the year 1929. A young scientist named W. C. Pei unearthed a skullcap in a limestone cave near the village of Zhoukoudian, not far from China's capital of Beijing. Since then five skullcaps and fossil bones of more than forty *erectus* individuals have been discovered. Originally they were called Peking Man.

Many more such bones have been lost over the years as

Olduvai Gorge in Tanzania, Africa, has yielded a remarkable treasure trove of human prehistory dating between 2 million and 1 million years ago. The gorge is an ancient ravine about 300 feet (90 meters) deep cut into the Great Rift Valley of East Africa. The world-renowned anthropologists Louis S. B. Leakey and his wife, Mary, made numerous important fossil finds in the gorge over a period of 50 years.

farmers searching through the limestone caves have made off with them. The bones have been ground up as powder, called "dragon bones," and sold to superstitious people as a cure for just about any known disease. This practice with animal bones—especially with the horns of the endangered black rhinoceros—continues to this day in China. More bones of Peking Man have also been found at sites named Lantian and Hexian.

Interestingly, the original Peking Man bones mysteriously disappeared in 1941, during World War II. To prevent the precious bones from being stolen by invading Japanese soldiers, the scientist in charge of the bones packed them up for shipment to the United States for safekeeping. But the bones vanished before they ever reached the ship. All that remains of the original Peking Man are plaster casts, although the casts are very faithful reproductions.

Peking Man lived more than 400,000 years ago and may be the ancestors of modern Asian people. At least archaeologist Jia Lanpo, who led excavations in the Zhoukoudian caves in the 1930s, thinks so. He points out that the nose bone of Peking Man was low and that the cheeks were flat, which is true with Asian people today. Lanpo further thinks that the ancestors of all humans living today are to be found in Asia, not Africa.

Still Older Asians

Still older human remains have been uncovered in China. A piece of jawbone and two teeth found at the Longgupo cave site in Szechwan Province have been dated at 1.9 million years old, but some scientists are doubtful about the dates. Others think the teeth may be from an ape and not a human. But in Yunnan Province human teeth and tools have definitely been dated back to 1.8 million years. And if you travel westward out of China into

Russia's Republic of Georgia, archaeologists will show you a lower human jaw found in 1991 that they say belonged to an *erectus* individual who lived more than 1.6 million years ago. Again, that is the time of the Turkana Boy in Africa. Some question the age of the jaw, saying that it is much younger.

Next, if you travel southward from Georgia into Israel you will be shown the Ubeidiya site, near the Sea of Galilee. More than ten thousand stone tools, including hand axes are there, along with animal fossils. The animal remains have been dated at 1.4 million years old. The site ranks as one of the oldest *erectus* finds outside of Africa.

New finds in the Chinese province of Hubei in 1990 seem to show that *erectus* groups differed noticeably from each other from place to place. In other words, there were different races of *erectus*, says paleoanthropologist Dennis Etler, of the University of California at Berkeley.

A recent and surprising find in Indonesia makes the picture of *erectus* even more puzzling. Swisher has come up with an age of 50,000 years for *erectus* fossils dug up at Ngandong in the 1930s. Earlier the fossils were thought to be from 100,000 to 300,000 years old. This means that *Homo erectus* must have lived side by side with *Homo sapiens*, now believed to have been living in Indonesia some 70,000 years ago.

It now seems certain that *Homo erectus* (including *ergaster*) originated some 2 million years ago and by 1.8 million years ago had spread to several other parts of the world. Our task now is to push the anthropological clock back even further. For now we want to find out where *Homo erectus* (*ergaster*) came from. Who were *their* parents?

Seven

Africa's Human Fossil Gold Mine

A Handy Man

The gold mine of human fossils is Olduvai Gorge in East Africa. Paleoanthropologist Louis S. B. Leakey began digging there in 1931. Since then thousands of ancient human and prehuman remains have been unearthed and have added tremendously to our knowledge of our origins. The son of British missionaries, Leakey was convinced that our origins were to be found in Africa and would turn out to be very ancient. Today few doubt that he was right.

Olduvai Gorge is a 328-foot deep (100-meter-deep) canyon carved out by a river long ago. About 25 miles (40 kilometers) long, its walls are layers of time going back some 2 million years. At first Leakey and his wife, Mary, found crude stone tools flaked from pebbles and called choppers. Their dream was to find the makers of those ancient tools.

The earliest known species deserving of the description "human" is Homo habilis, meaning "handy man." A toolmaker, Homo habilis was first discovered by the Leakeys in 1960. This human ancestor lived from 2.5 to 1.6 million years ago.

In 1960 that dream came true when Leakey, his wife, and son Jonathan found pieces of a skull, jaw, and hand. At the time it was the most important find in the history of our family tree. It pinpointed the oldest member of the genus *Homo*, the first true human creature. It was named *Homo habilis*, meaning "handy man," who lived from 2.5 to 1.6 million years ago.

What was *habilis* like? Many scientists are convinced that evolution sometimes plods along slowly over millions of years. Then other times it spurts ahead and brings about dramatic change over much shorter periods. That seems to have been the case with *habilis*. Suddenly we find a creature with a brain size of 650 milliliters, half again larger than their ancestors. The brain also included, for the first time, an area that involved speech. Another *habilis* skull dug up in 1973 at the Koobi Fora site had a size of 510 milliliters. Since then still more *habilis* remains have been found.

Nutcracker Man

Homo habilis lived during busy times, for he was not alone. On a July morning in 1959 Mary Leakey came running into camp and shouted to her husband, "I've got him! I've got him!" The "him" turned out to be more than four hundred bone fragments, which they were able to glue together as the skull of an adult ape-man 1.8 million years old. Its face was so massive and its teeth so large that they called him "Nutcracker Man," but he was put into a new genus and given the scientific name *Australopithecus boisei*. His brain size was 530 milliliters (1.1 pints), about the same as that of *habilis*. It turned out that *boisei*, who lived in eastern Africa, was an evolutionary dead end. They appeared on the scene about 2.1 million years ago, then the species simply died out 1.7 million years ago. This meant that *habilis* had a neighbor.

In fact, *habilis* had several neighbors, but just how many is unknown. It seems that *erectus* (*ergaster*) lived when *habilis* did. Another was *Australopithecus robustus*, who lived in southern Africa from 2 to 1.6 million years ago. The fossil remains of about

Called the "ultimate chewing machine" because of its powerful jaws and huge grinding teeth, Australopithecus robustus was a neighbor of H. habilis. Robustus roamed over South Africa from 2 million years ago and survived for a little more than a half million years. They seem to have used bone and wood tools, but no worked-stone tools have been found with them. A study of their teeth shows that robustus people didn't live much past age seventeen.

130 *robustus* individuals have been found in caves near Swartkrans, South Africa. One of the skulls was that of a child. It had two perfectly round holes in it, possibly made by a leopard that discovered the dead child, sunk its teeth into the eye sockets and back of the skull, and so carried it off.

Robustus individuals had massive heads with large faces and powerful jaws with huge grinding teeth. They have been called "the ultimate chewing machine." Their vegetarian diet included nuts, fruits, roots, and tubers. They seem to have used bone and wood tools, but no worked stone tools have been found with them. A study of their teeth shows that *robustus* people didn't live much past age seventeen. They appear in the fossil record some 2 million years ago and survived for a little more than a half million years. Their brain size was some 530 milliliters (1.1 pints). Still another of *habilis*'s neighbors was *Australopithecus aethiopicus*, who lived in eastern Africa from 2.6 to 2.2 million years ago. These creatures were larger than *habilis* and her other two neighbors. They, too, were evolutionary dead ends.

We have reached a point in our backward journey through the ages to a time when several upright walking species were roaming the land. Possibly they interacted; possibly they fought. We just don't know. Exactly how many different species there were we don't know. We can say little about how they walked and which of them made tools. Many of the answers lie buried in the ground. Year by year, bit by bit, we are prying them out.

Although we have introduced the genus *Australopithecus* (meaning "southern ape") in this chapter, their real story hasn't yet begun in our account. For it was *Australopithecus africanus* that many paleoanthropologists claim as our prehuman ancestors. Let us now examine our "southern ape" relatives, who gave rise to *Homo habilis*.

Eight

The Southern Apes

The "Beat-up Chimpanzee"

In 1924 miners in South Africa blasted open a cave in search of lime. One of them noticed part of a fossil skull that had long been encased in sand, rocks, and lime all cemented together. The boss of the mining operation packed the fossil in a box and sent it to Professor Raymond Dart, head of the Anatomy Department at Witwatersrand. It didn't take Dart long to realize that he was gazing on "one of the most significant finds ever made in the history of anthropology," he later wrote.

How Old Is That Bone?
Layers of volcanic ash deposited and turned to stone at various times over the past 4 or so million years give scientists a way of dating teeth, jaw, skull, and other bone fragments. Rushing water cuts deep valleys into the land and so carves out a profile of the layers of sediments to a depth of hundreds of feet. Although the sediments and fossil bone fragments they may hold may not be dated directly, the volcanic ash layers can be

The fossil was that of a five- or six-year-old child who died between 1 and 2 million years earlier. Dart, age thirty-two at the time, became famous overnight for his find, but not without some ridicule. One anthropologist scoffed at the fossil, calling it "just a somewhat beat-up chimpanzee."

A dozen years later a Scottish anthropologist named Robert Broom uncovered an adult skull just like Dart's Taung Cave child about 30 miles (48 kilometers) west of Johannesburg. From time to time Broom bought fossil remains from the manager of the lime quarry at Sterkfontein. The manager was secretive about

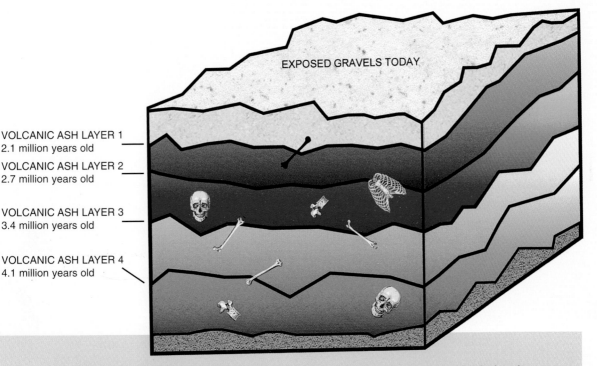

EXPOSED GRAVELS TODAY

VOLCANIC ASH LAYER 1
2.1 million years old

VOLCANIC ASH LAYER 2
2.7 million years old

VOLCANIC ASH LAYER 3
3.4 million years old

VOLCANIC ASH LAYER 4
4.1 million years old

dated very accurately. So if a fossil bone, for instance, is found in a layer of ash dated at 2.1 million years old, then the bone most likely also is that age. An exposed skull fragment found between ash Layer 2 and ash Layer 3 must be somewhere between 2.7 and 3.4 million years old. Human fossil remains more than 4 million years old have been dated by using uranium-238 atomic clocks.

where he got the fossils, but eventually he told Broom that they came from a schoolboy who lived nearby. Broom found the boy, who showed him four beautiful fossil teeth. Later the boy took Broom to his favorite fossil site and produced "a beautiful lower jaw with two teeth in position," Broom later wrote. More such fragments proved to be additional fossils like those found by Dart. He named these ancient creatures *Australopithecus africanus*, meaning "southern ape of Africa."

The *africanus* individuals found in southern Africa seemed to be about 3 million years old, but accurate dating is hard to do. The area lacks volcanic ash layers that can be dated accurately, so less reliable methods have been used.

Meet Lucy

Just as Dart's discovery of the Taung child shook anthropology to its roots, a discovery made in 1974 caused an even greater stir. In November of that year paleoanthropologist Donald C. Johanson, of the Institute of Human Origins in Berkeley, California, and his graduate student Tom Gray unearthed a remarkable fossil skeleton. The find pushed the date of the then earliest known *hominids* back to 3.2 million years. Hominids are creatures who go back more than 4 million years and include all the species we have described so far, including us. All hominids walk upright.

The place was Hadar, in North Africa's Ethiopia. The skeleton was that of a female who stood 3 feet 8 inches (112 centimeters) tall and weighed about 65 pounds (29 kilograms). She had a mixture of ape and human features. "Her long arms dangled apelike by her side," Johanson later wrote in *National Geographic* magazine. They named her Lucy, after the Beatles song, "Lucy in the Sky with Diamonds." The scientific name they

The Beatles song "Lucy in the Sky with Diamonds" provided the name for the small female hominid unearthed by Donald C. Johanson in Ethiopia in 1974. The find pushed the date of the then earliest known hominids back to 3.2 million years. When alive, Lucy weighed about 65 pounds (30 kilograms). Her scientific name is Australopithecus afarensis. Lucy had a mixture of ape and human features, as shown in an artist's version of what her kind might have looked like when alive.

gave her was *Australopithecus afarensis*, meaning "southern ape of Afar."

Since Lucy was more apelike than humanlike, we will refer to her kind as hominids rather than as "people." Scientists believe that Lucy and her companions gave rise to all other hominids after her.

The Lucy bones collected and assembled by Johanson contained about 40 percent of her skeleton, but the skull was missing. In 1992 Johanson was lucky enough to find an *afarensis* skull, which helped complete the story of Lucy. She had a jutting jaw, a large brow ridge over the eyes, and wide cheeks with strong facial muscles. Based on other *afarensis* finds, paleoanthropologists now think these hominids lived almost unchanged for 900,000 years. Lucy roamed the countryside a million years or more before the Taung child did.

Like her *africanus* offspring, Lucy had large back teeth. Her forehead was low, her nose flat like that of a gorilla, and she had no chin to speak of. Recall that prominent chins were not to evolve until *Homo sapiens* times, much later. The brain size of *afarensis* was between 375 to 500 milliliters (0.80 to 1 pint), fairly close to that of *Homo habilis*. Lucy and her relatives probably lacked the brain area associated with speech, so these hominids most likely communicated by grunts and gestures. They seem to have traveled in packs of twenty-five to thirty individuals. Always they had to be on the lookout for saber-toothed cats and other animals. Lucy's type were not organized hunters, or predators. They lacked tools and did not know how to control fire. Their lives at night must have been especially frightening, always being on guard against prowling animals. They may even have taken to the trees for protection, but they were much less able tree climbers than apes, and their stride lacked the grace of later humans.

In 1978 Mary Leakey discovered two sets of fossil footprints preserved in volcanic ash turned to stone at Laetoli, in Africa's Tanzania. Careful study of the prints showed they were made by an individual 4 feet 8 inches (142 centimeters) tall and a slightly shorter companion. Later fossil bones were found in the ash layer of the footprints. They were dated at 3.56 million years old. Johanson says the Laetoli bones come from the same *afarensis* species as his Hadar fossils. Others are not so sure.

Expeditions to other Ethiopian sites in 1982 uncovered more *afarensis* fossils. The expeditions' leaders were Desmond Clark and Tim White, of the University of California at Berkeley. They found skull and upper leg bone fragments. White said that the pelvis and leg bone pieces clearly showed that Lucy and her clan walked the way we do. Further, their limbs were not specialized for an apelike life in the trees. These fossils were dated at close to 4 million years old. Johanson feels that Lucy's *afarensis* species is the one that gave rise to several other hominid types, but that only one evolved into our human ancestors of the genus *Homo*.

First a New Species . . .

For a while it looked as though Lucy was the oldest hominid, but she was to be toppled from her pedestal. In 1994 Meave Leakey, Mary's daughter-in-law, excavated a site called Kanapoi, which lies near the southern end of Lake Turkana. Three large teeth had been found there. They were very apelike and turned out to be from a hominid type that seemed to bridge the gap between true apes and *afarensis* hominids.

Leakey's team scoured the area. First they cleared away the larger pebbles, then shoveled the loose soil through a screen. This turned up an almost complete set of teeth from the creature's lower jaw. Based on the age of the volcanic ash in the sediments containing the teeth, they have been dated at 4.1 million years old. That was 600,000 years older than Lucy. The apelike owner of the teeth was so much more primitive than *afarensis* that Leakey assigned it a new species, *Australopithecus anamensis*.

A hominid even older than Lucy? For a while it looked as though Lucy was the oldest hominid, but in 1994 she was toppled from her pedestal by Meave Leakey's discovery of still older hominid remains near the southern end of East Africa's Lake Turkana. Leakey discovered an almost complete set of lower jaw teeth of an early hominid that turned out to be 4.1 million years old. The teeth were very apelike and seemed to bridge the gap between true apes and afarensis hominids.

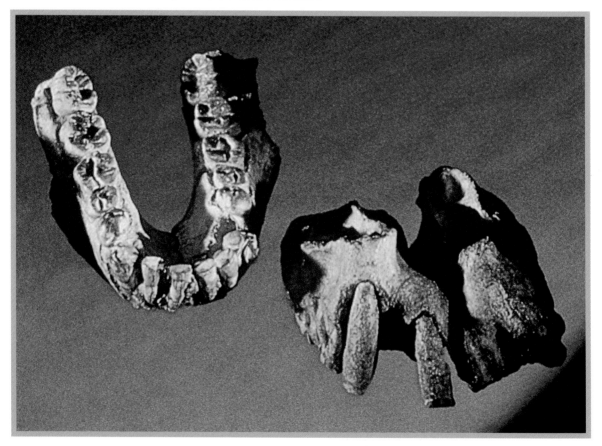

To date, a total of fifty-nine *anamensis* fossil bones have been found. They suggest a mix between chimplike and human-like features. Two sections of the large lower leg bone clearly show that it walked upright. However, the smaller leg bone shows that the animal probably was better than *afarensis* at grasping objects with its longer and slightly curved toes. Did these hominids spend part of their time in the trees? Fossil hand bones from a 3.5-million-year-old hominid had been found earlier at the Turkwel site, farther north. The bones show signs of big tendons that controlled very strong curved fingers well designed for climbing trees. A complete skeleton would help tell if *anamensis* was just as well, or even better, equipped. Leakey says that her hominid had some features common to hominids but other features common to chimpanzees, our closest relatives.

. . . Then a New Genus

Meave Leakey's record for the oldest hominid was even shorter lived than Lucy's record. Also in 1994, Tim White, of the University of California at Berkeley, turned up an even older hominid while digging at the Aramis site in Ethiopia. White's hominid was dated at 4.4 million years old. Teeth and arm bones showed that the animal walked upright. Soon afterward, parts of a lower leg bone and the pelvis of another individual were found. White thought that this animal was different enough, and still more primitive, to be put in a new genus. He named it *Ardipithecus ramidus*, meaning "ground ape, root." Leakey feels that her Kanapoi fossils may belong to Lucy's ancestors and that White's Aramis fossils may belong on a different branch of the hominid family tree. Again, no one knows how many species fill the gap between true apes and the first true hominids, but each year new fossil finds are helping us to find out.

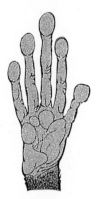
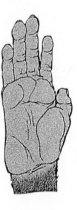

TREE SHREW   LEMUR   TARSIER   MONKEY

Similarity in structure among related groups of animals is convincing evidence that they all evolved from a common ancestor. Long claws in tree shrews evolved into nails in monkeys, apes, and humans. Notice the large finger pads of lemurs and tarsiers. The hands of all six of these primates are specialized for grasping, as clearly shown in the photograph of the hand of an orangutan, a great ape (left).

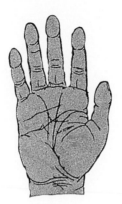

CHIMPANZEE   HUMAN

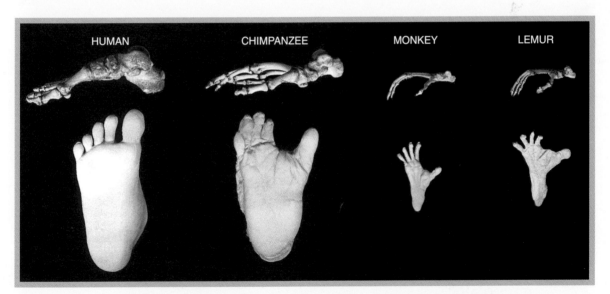

*The human foot evolved in a way that permitted an upright posture. A larg-
er heel and stronger foot arch enable humans to walk upright and flat-foot-
ed. Weaker arch bones and smaller heels cause apes to walk on the outer
sides of their feet. Notice the wide gap between the big toe and the rest of
the foot in chimpanzees, monkeys, and lemurs. These handlike feet do the
special job of grasping that is needed for life in the trees.*

61

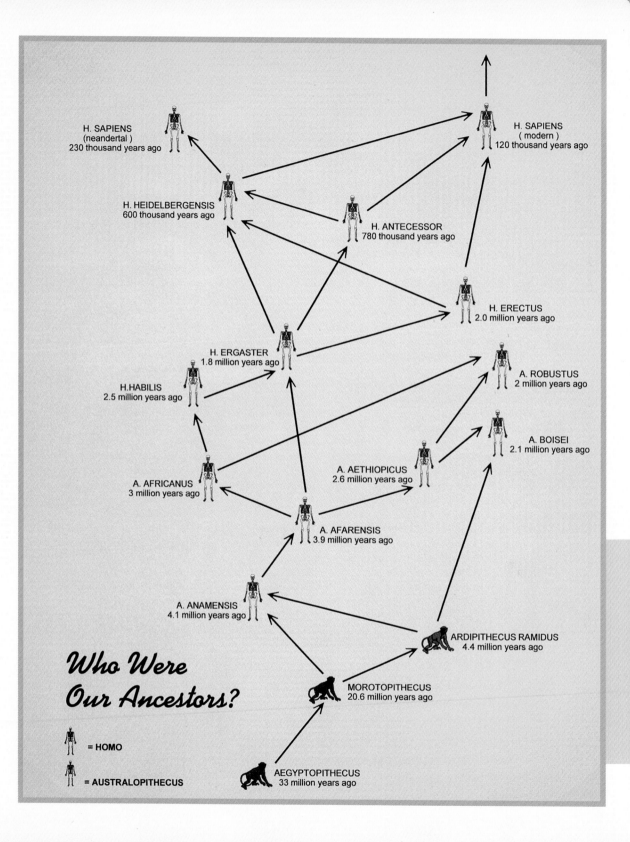

Who Were Our Ancestors?

Nine

How Far Back Do We Go?

Dawn Ape

In their attempts to trace our human origins back through time, paleoanthropologists are faced with many burning questions: we will consider two here. First, who were our ancestors some 5 million and more years ago?

Scientists raking over ancient fossil remains in what is now Africa's sprawling Sahara sands have painstakingly pieced together bones of a creature that lived 33 million years ago.

Identifying fossil remains of our ancestors from a few hundred thousand to millions of years ago is one thing. Putting them in some sort of order to account for which family member gave rise to this or that new member is quite a different matter. For example, did a relatively new fossil find named Homo antecessor *give rise to* H. sapiens, *or was it* H. erectus *or* H. heidelbergensis *that evolved into our species? Many similar questions can be asked all along the maze of hominid evolution. Note that all* Australopithecus *members are shown in the same color, as are all the* Homo *members. The three oldest members at the bottom of the chart are given separate colors since we cannot be sure of their lines of development. Each time you are introduced to a new member of our ancestral family tree, refer to this chart to find out where that member may have come from and where it may have led.*

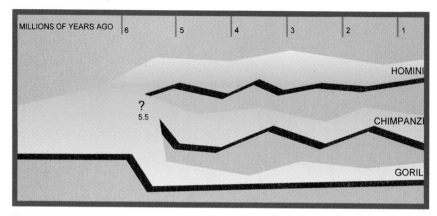

MILLIONS OF YEARS AGO 6 5 4 3 2 1

HOMINI

?
5.5

CHIMPANZI

GORIL

Sometime around 5.5 million years ago animals that were at home in trees swung down and took up life on the ground. By the time they began to develop the habit of walking upright, they had a pelvis and limbs that allowed a course of evolution markedly different from our closest relatives, chimpanzees and gorillas. In short, they gave rise to our hominid line.

Nicknamed "Dawn Ape," its scientific name is *Aegyptopithecus*, meaning "Egypt ape." Those many million years ago the Sahara region was tropical forest, and our 9-pound (4-kilogram) Dawn Ape scrambled among the branches. Its teeth were apelike, and its limbs monkeylike. Elwyn Simons, of Duke University, thinks that Dawn Ape is the "oldest creature we know that is in the direct ancestry of man."

What happened over the following millions of years to the time of the first hominids is a haze of mystery. Fossil remains of some half dozen apelike creatures that lived between 20 and 8 million years ago have been turned up. But the scanty finds offer too little for us to draw detailed pictures of what went on. Even so, we can make some intelligent guesses. Based on the two oldest finds so far—Leakey's Kanapoi find and White's Aramis find—we can imagine the ancestors of those ancient hominids a few million years earlier.

They were certainly apelike, lived in then-forested East Africa, and were at home in the trees. As their fossils turn up, we will almost certainly find signs of stout shoulders, long and powerful arms with well-curved fingers for grasping and swinging from tree branches. And we can expect to find a pelvis more typical of an ape than of a creature that walked along on two legs. Then something happened. Some of those apelike creatures came down out of the trees and took up life on the ground. Perhaps they spent part of the time in the trees and part experimenting with walking upright. A 20.6-million-year-old apelike creature has been found in Uganda and placed in the new genus *Morotopithecus*, meaning "Moroto ape," after the Uganda site's

The oldest creature in the line of descendants of humans is now thought to be one called "Dawn Ape," or Aegyptopithecus zeuxis. Its fossil skull remains were found in the Egyptian desert and dated at about 33 million years old. As pictured by an artist, the small primate may have given rise to both monkeys and apes. It lived at a time when northern Egypt was tropical rain forest instead of desert.

name. The creature may be a tree-climbing ancestor of living apes, hominids, and gibbons, but it is too soon to tell. Sometime between 5 and 7 million years ago, the hominids took one evolutionary path, and the apes took another.

Down Out of the Trees

The second burning question is: What made our apelike ancestors come down out of the trees and take up life on the grassy plains? Before 6 million years ago the climate in Africa had been mostly

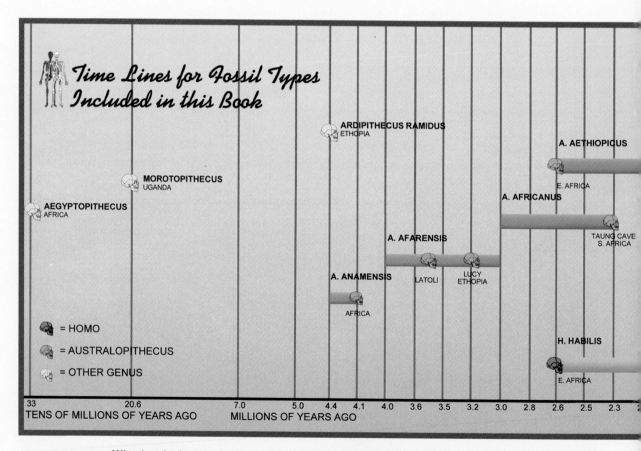

Time Lines for Fossil Types Included in this Book

ARDIPITHECUS RAMIDUS
ETHOPIA

A. AETHIOPICUS

MOROTOPITHECUS
UGANDA

E. AFRICA

A. AFRICANUS

AEGYPTOPITHECUS
AFRICA

A. AFARENSIS

TAUNG CAVE
S. AFRICA

A. ANAMENSIS

LATOLI

LUCY
ETHOPIA

AFRICA

= HOMO

= AUSTRALOPITHECUS

= OTHER GENUS

H. HABILIS

E. AFRICA

| 33 | 20.6 | 7.0 | 5.0 | 4.4 | 4.1 | 4.0 | 3.6 | 3.5 | 3.2 | 3.0 | 2.8 | 2.6 | 2.5 | 2.3 |

TENS OF MILLIONS OF YEARS AGO   MILLIONS OF YEARS AGO

Who lived when is shown in this time line extending from modern humans (upper right) to fossils dated back to some 33 million years ago. The length of each time line represents the presently known span of time that various types evolved and survived before dying out or evolving into new species.

As the evolutionary pathways leading to modern humans (see page 62)

warm for millions of years. But then it changed dramatically over the next million years. It became cooler by about 10 Fahrenheit degrees. That caused a rapid buildup of ice in Antarctica. It also caused sea levels around the world to lower by nearly 200 feet (61 meters) as more and more ocean water evaporated, fell as snow, and then became locked up as ice. Africa's drier and cooler climate caused the forests to retreat and gave rise to vast grasslands, like those in East Africa today.

The change in environment was too much for many of the

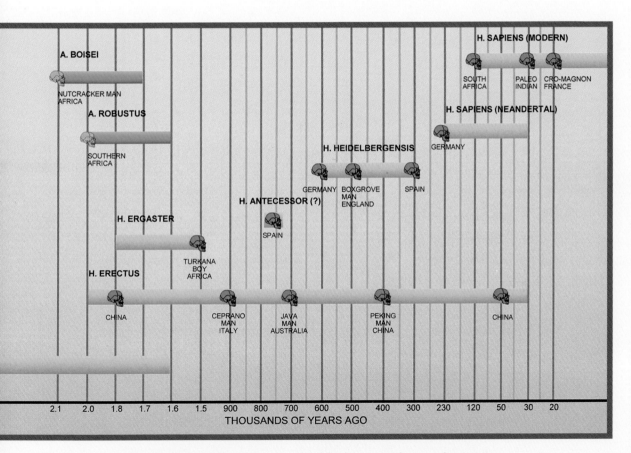

are continually being updated by new fossil finds, so are the time lines estimating when our ancestors lived.

Almost every year anthropologists working in different parts of the world dig up new fossils that make them rethink their ideas about the evolution of the human line.

forest dwellers, and they died out. Among them were species of forest antelope. But the sprawling grasslands offered new chances for the evolution of new species. For example, the first grazing antelopes appeared. We can read in the fossil record the extinction of some species and appearances of new ones in response to the new environment. One of those newcomers gave rise to the first hominids, and eventually to us.

Accounting for Race

Our species is the only hominid species that survived the many snares of extinction. Modern humans arrived on the scene between 100,000 and 200,000 years ago. Since that time our species has shown little change in anatomy. There are no other human species. But there are different peoples with different physical features in different geographical populations of *Homo sapiens*. We can see this in the relatively flat face of Chinese and Eskimos, the high cheekbones of Mongolians and certain ethnic groups of Siberia, and the long-limb anatomy of the Masai of Africa.

A race within any species can be thought of as a group of populations that have certain physical characteristics and genes in common. Human populations living in markedly different environments have adapted differently. The Eskimos' relatively short fingers are thought to be an adaptation to a cold environment. Short fingers have less surface area from which to lose heat and are less likely to get frostbitten than long ones. Inhabitants of the Andes Mountains of South America have evolved relatively large chests with larger lungs and more red blood cells than people living at sea level have. These features are *adaptations* to life at high altitude, where oxygen is harder to come by because of the lower atmospheric pressure. The dark

Racial differences are commonly expressed as physical features that set one group of populations apart from another. Examples are the Masai of Kenya, Africa. They have uncommonly long limbs that give them spectacular dancing ability, including high leaps. In contrast is the short Evenk woman from northern Siberia. High cheekbones, short fingers, and Eskimo-like features characterize her people.

skin of Africans may be an adaptation to protect the skin from the damaging action of ultraviolet radiation. Such radiation is stronger near the equator than it is in middle and high latitudes.

It is hard to pin down the origin of certain *variations*—skin color, blood type, face structure, for example—that have been used to place various populations of people into races. The history of racial distinctions goes back many centuries. It includes biologists Franz Weidenerich's and Carleton Coon's idea that the modern human races descended from old hominid lines that evolved independently into different racial groups: a Middle East type, perhaps Mount Carmel Man, supposedly led to the Caucasoid (white-skinned) race; Rhodesian Man to the Negroid (black-skinned) race; Peking Man to the Mongoloid (high cheekbones and yellow-skinned) race; Java Man to the Australoid (brown-skinned) race; and the American Indians to the Amerinds (red-skinned) race. The idea that today's human geographical races have evolved from populations' adaptations over thousands of years is hard to challenge, even if some of the causes are not clear.

Some populations keep themselves pretty much isolated and so tend to keep their characteristics. Africa's Pygmies are an example. Such groups usually resist breeding with individuals from populations different from their own. Population "barriers," such as climate extremes, sometimes act as geographical fences that keep a population pretty much to itself. But cultural forces also can isolate certain small, local populations. For example, certain religious sects discourage marriage outside their group. But the tendency today in many parts of the world is to mix the races rather than keep them separate. This is especially true in the world's large cities, where mixed populations are the rule.

Mixing the races through interbreeding tends to blur racial differences. For instance, the Hawaiians, once a genetically and culturally distinct group, have all but lost their original identity. Their homeland is a vast melting pot of Westerners, Chinese, Japanese, Hawaiian, and other nationalities and cultures. The same is happening in many parts of the world. The causes are changing social values, rapid communication of ideas, and the ease of crossing distances of several thousand miles in only a few hours.

Some biologists feel that the blurring of racial differences makes it increasingly hard—and misleading—to place certain individuals into this or that neat racial compartment. For that reason they have given up using the term race as it applies to humans.

To encourage its members to avoid earlier, and false, notions about "race," the American Association of Physical Anthropologists has drawn up a set of guidelines. Among those guidelines are the following:

- *"Pure" races in the human family, in the sense of a group of populations all having the same genetic makeup, do not exist. And there is no evidence that they have ever existed.*

- *There are obvious physical differences between populations living in different geographic regions. Some of those differences are strongly inherited. Others come from differences in nutrition, way of life, and other influences of the environment.*

- *Human beings cannot be classified into neat categories with boundaries fixed for all time.*

- *It is meaningless from a biological point of view to say this or that race is inferior or superior to any other race.*

- *Local populations linked by certain physical and genetic features are continually coming into and passing out of existence.*

- *Cultural characteristics have nothing to do with genetic inheritance.*

- *There is no national, religious, language, or cultural group or economic class that can be called a "race."*

Our Future Evolution?

Will *Homo sapiens* keep evolving, as the group has in the past? Paleoanthropologist Ian Tattersall, of The American Museum of Natural History in New York, thinks not. He gives two reasons. First, a rapidly growing world population is causing a mixing of many local populations. Second, people can easily and speedily migrate from one part of the world to another, and are doing so. Both activities cause a blurring of the uniqueness of populations. Such conditions simply are not the right fuel to keep the wheels of human evolution turning. "The conditions for significant evolutionary change simply don't exist," he says.

It is hard to deny that human beings have evolved from earlier hominid groups, which in turn evolved from common ancestors going back more than 30 million years.

The convincing evidence is the fossil record. What is less clear are the exact routes that human evolution has followed over the past five, ten, twenty million years. But each year new fossil finds add to the ever-growing body of evidence. As they do, our knowledge of our evolutionary past is enriched, and our view of that fascinating past is brought into sharper focus. The answers are there in the ground, waiting to be unearthed by those who want to know. And the answers are bound to change some of our thinking today.

Adaptation—A trait within a plant or animal population that makes it more suited for its environment.

Anatomy—The science of the shape and structure of organisms.

Anthropology—The "study of man," including social organization, customs and beliefs, language, and physical aspects of people who are living today and who lived long ago.

Archaeology—The discovery and interpretation of material remains left by peoples who lived in the past.

Climate—A region's weather averaged over a long span of time. From the Greek word *klima*, meaning "slope" or "incline," and referring to the *degree* of slant of the Sun's rays relative to Earth's surface.

Cro-Magnon—Early *Homo sapiens* who were more modern than and replaced the Neandertals about 30,000 years ago. They had a rich culture and left many beautiful cave paintings in France and Spain.

Culture—The customs, equipment, techniques, manufactures, ideas, language, and beliefs of a people.

Erosion—The long-term effects of heat, water, wind, ice, and acid rain that may chip away or chemically dissolve solid rock. The chipped-away particles are called sediments. Sediments may be formed by mechanical action or by chemical or biochemical processes.

Evolution—The various patterns of biological change that ultimately cause the success (adaptation) or failure (extinction) of species and produce new species of plants and animals. As it has in the past, biological evolution continues to take place today. Charles Darwin is credited with developing the basic principles of evolution.

Extinction—The total disappearance of an entire species of plants or animals. Once a species has become extinct, it is gone forever.

Fossils—The remains of once-living plants or animals. Fossils may be bits of bone or teeth or even footprints or other imprints left from long ago. Most fossils are found in sedimentary rock and usually are more than 10,000 years old.

Gene—That biological unit of inheritance that determines a particular trait, such as hair color, height, and general physical appearance of an individual.

Genus—A broad grouping of organisms, all of which have certain characteristics in common but which belong to different species. For example, there are various species of the genus *Homo. Homo sapiens* refers to modern humans, while *Homo habilis* refers to a humanlike species that lived long ago.

Geologic Time—The time that has passed since Earth's history began some 4.6 billion years ago.

Hominid—Any member of the human family that walks upright on two legs. Modern humans are the only surviving hominids. A group known as *Australopithecus* may have been the first true hominids; they lived as long ago as about 4 million years.

Homo erectus—A group of hominids who were clearly human but not yet modern humans. *Homo erectus* hunted, lived in caves, and knew the art of starting fire. The name means "upright man."

Homo habilis—A humanlike species who lived in Africa and Asia some 2.5 to 1.5 million years ago and gave rise to *Homo erectus.*

Homo sapiens—The group name of modern humans. It means "wise man."

Ice Age—Any extended period of time during which a substantial portion of Earth's surface is covered by "permanent" ice. There have been seven known major ice ages during the past 700,000 years, with the last ice age reaching its peak about 18,000 years ago.

Mutation—A chance change in a plant or animal's genes that makes the organism different from its parents. Most mutations are harmful, although many prove beneficial. Mutations may be passed on from parents to offspring.

Neandertal—Large-jawed people who lived across Europe into the Near East and into central Asia. About 5 feet tall (152 centimeters), they were strong and had large bones. They became extinct about 30,000 years ago.

Paleoanthropologist—An anthropologist who studies the physical features and cultures of ancient peoples in an attempt to trace the evolution of human beings.

Paleontology—The science concerned with the study fossils of life forms that have existed throughout geologic time.

Paleontologist—A scientist who specializes in the recovery and study of fossils.

Race—Some biologists feel that the blurring of racial differences makes it increasingly hard—and misleading—to place certain individuals into this or that neat racial compartment. For that reason they have given up using the term race as it applies to humans.

Sediments—The loose bits and pieces of clay, mud, sand, gravel, lime, and other earth materials that pile up century after century and become squeezed by the great weight of new sediments above. Eventually such sediment heaps may be thrust up as new mountains.

Species—Any one kind of animal or plant group, each member of which is like every other member in certain important ways. All populations of such a group are capable of interbreeding and producing healthy offspring.

Variation—The racial and certain other differences among the individuals making up a population—height, eye and hair color, for example. These variations are what lead to evolutionary change.

Further Reading

"AAPA Statement on Biological Aspects of Race." *American Journal of Physical Anthropology*, vol. 101 (4) (December 1996) pp. 569–570.

Bower, Bruce. "Oldest Fossil Ape May Be Human Ancestor." *Science News* (April 19, 1997) p. 239.

——————— "Pruning the Family Tree," *Science News* (September 2, 1995) pp. 154–155.

Brainard, Jeffrey. "Giving Neandertals Their Due." *Science News* (August 1, 1998) pp. 72–74.

Cartmill, Matt. "The Gift of Gab." *Discover* (November 1998) pp. 56–64.

Flanagan, Ruth. "Out of Africa." *Earth* (February 1996) pp. 26–35.

Gallant, Roy A. *Before the Sun Dies: the Story of Evolution*. New York: Macmillan, 1989.

——————— *Fossils*. New York: Franklin Watts, 1985.

——————— *How Life Began*. New York: Four Winds Press, 1975.

Gore, Rick. "Expanding Worlds." The Dawn of Humans Series, *National Geographic* (May 1997) pp. 84–109.

——————— "The First Europeans." The Dawn of Humans Series, *National Geographic* (July 1997) pp. 96–113.

——————— "The First Steps." The Dawn of Humans Series, *National Geographic* (February 1997) pp. 72–99.

——————— "Neandertals." The Dawn of Humans Series, *National Geographic* (January 1996) pp. 2–35.

_____ "Tracking the first of Our Kind." The Dawn of Humans Series, *National Geographic* (September 1997) pp. 92–99.

Johanson, Donald C. "Face-to-Face with Lucy's Family." The Dawn of Humans Series, *National Geographic* (March 1996) pp. 96–117.

_____ and Blake Edgar. "From Lucy to Language." *Earth* (June 1997) pp. 40–47.

Leakey, Meave. "The Farthest Horizon." The Dawn of Humans Series, *National Geographic* (September 1995) pp. 38–51.

_____ and Alan Walker. "Early Hominid Fossils from Africa." *Scientific American* (June 1997) pp.74–79.

Lewin, Roger. *In the Age of Mankind*. Washington, D.C.: Smithsonian Books, 1988.

Putnam, John J. "The Search for Modern Humans." The Dawn of Humans Series, *National Geographic* (October 1988) pp. 439–481.

Rigaud, Jean-Philippe. "Art Treasures from the Ice Age: Lascaux Cave." The Dawn of Humans Series, *National Geographic* (October 1988) pp. 482–499.

Tattersall, Ian. *The Fossil Trail*. New York: Oxford, 1995.

_____ "Out of Africa Again . . . and Again." *Scientific American* (April 1997) pp.60–67.

Tudge, Colin. "The Future Evolution of *Homo Sapiens*." *Earth* (February 1996) pp. 36–40.

Weaver, Kenneth F. "The Search for Our Ancestors." The Dawn of Humans Series, *National Geographic* (November 1985) pp. 560–629.

Wolpoff, Milford, and Rachel Caspari. *Race and Human Evolution*. New York: Simon & Schuster, 1997.

Index

Page numbers for illustrations are in **boldface**.